Blonde Jo

A Huge Collection Of Dumb Blonde Jokes

By Charlie Crapper

Funny Blonde Jokes

These funny blonde jokes will give you plenty to smile about. We have many pearls of wisdom to share with you, so brace yourself for plenty of laughs with this huge collection of dumb blonde jokes.

This huge collection of ditzy blonde jokes and dumb blonde jokes will have you laughing out loud. The funny blonde jokes in this book feature a number of one-liners, plenty of quick fire question and answer style gags, many story based jokes and there is even a chapter on chat up lines to use on blondes.

This book has well over 250 blonde jokes, in what could possibly be the funniest blonde jokes ever.

Published by Glowworm Press
7 Nuffield Way
Abingdon OX14 1RL

Copyright

All rights reserved. No part of this publication may be reproduced in any form or by any means without the written permission of the publisher. The information herein is offered for informational purposes only, and is universal as so. The presentation of the information is without contract or any type of guarantee assurance. Under no circumstances will any legal responsibility or blame be held against the author for any reparation, damages or monetary loss due to the information herein, either directly or indirectly.

FOREWORD

When I was asked to write a foreword to this book I was extremely flattered.

That is until I was told that I was the completely last resort by the author, Charlie Crapper, and that everyone else he had approached had said they couldn't or wouldn't do it!

I have known Charlie for a number of years and his ability to create funny jokes is incredible. He is quick witted and an expert at crafting clever puns and amusing gags and as he has a real soft spot for dumb blondes, I feel he is the ideal man to put together a joke book about blondes.

He will be glad you have bought this book, as he has an expensive lifestyle to maintain.

Lady Luck

Table of Contents

Chapter 1: One Liner Blonde Jokes

Chapter 2: Question and Answer Blonde Jokes

Chapter 3: Short Blonde Jokes

Chapter 4: Longer Blonde Jokes

Chapter 5: Rude Q&A Blonde Jokes

Chapter 6: Rude Blonde Jokes

Chapter 7: You Know You Are Blonde Gags

Chapter 8: Blonde Pick-Up Lines

Chapter 9: About The Author

Chapter 1: One Liner Blonde Jokes

Three blondes walk into a building. You'd think at least one of them would have seen it.

Did you hear about the blonde that went to the library and checked out a book called "How to Hug". When she got home, she found out it was volume twenty seven of an encyclopaedia.

My blonde girlfriend thought a quarterback was a refund.

Did you hear about the blonde skydiver? She missed the Earth.

Did you hear about the blonde who had a problem with her bed? She couldn't find a knife large enough to apply the bed spread.

Did you hear about the blonde tap dancer?

She fell in the sink.

Two blondes were driving to Disneyland, when they saw a sign that said "Disneyland left" so they started crying and headed home.

Did you hear about the blonde who gave her cat a bath? She still hasn't gotten all the hair off her tongue.

Did you hear about the blonde who gave birth to twins? Her husband is out looking for the other man.

Did you hear about the blonde mother who kept an icepack on her chest to keep the milk fresh?

A blonde sent a post card home. It said "Having a wonderful time. Where am I?"

Did you hear about the blonde who brought toilet paper to a craps game?

Did you hear about the new form of birth control for blondes? They take off their makeup.

Did you hear about the blonde who thought that intercourse was a state highway?

I got a compliment on my driving today a blonde said to her friend. "There was a note left on my windshield which said "parking fine".

Did you hear about the blonde coyote? She got stuck in a trap, chewed off three legs and was still stuck.

Did you hear about the blonde who thought that a sanitary belt was a shot from a clean whiskey glass?

Did you hear about the blonde who thought socialism meant partying.

If a blonde wants to learn to drive, it's best not to stand in her way.

Did you hear about the blonde who makes love cafeteria style? Everybody can help themselves.

Did you hear about the blonde who brought her cosmetics with her for a make-up exam?

Did you hear about the blonde who got caught stealing a calendar? She got twelve months.

Did you hear about the blonde with a PhD in Psychology? She'll blow your mind, too.

Did you hear about the blonde who thought Moby Dick was a sexually transmitted disease?

Chapter 2: Q&A Blonde Jokes

Q: Why did the blonde tip-toe past the medicine cabinet?

A: *So she wouldn't wake up the sleeping pills.*

Q: Why did the blonde shut herself in the fridge?

A: *She wanted to know if the light really goes off.*

Q: How can you make a blonde climb onto the roof?

A: *Tell her that drinks are on the house.*

Q: Why did the blonde get so excited after she finished her jigsaw puzzle in only 6 months?

A: *Because on the box it said "from 2-4 years".*

Q: How did the blonde die drinking milk?

A: *The cow fell on her.*

Q: How do you know a blonde has been using the computer?

A: *There is cheese in front of the mouse.*

Q: Why did eighteen blondes go to the movies together?

A: *They heard that under seventeen weren't admitted.*

Q: Why couldn't the blonde add 10 + 5 on a calculator?

A: *She couldn't find the "10" button.*

Q: Why is it wrong to say "a dumb blonde"?

A: *Because you don't say "a dead corpse" either, do you?*

Q: How are U.F.O.s and smart blondes alike?

A: *You keep hearing about them, but you never see them.*

Q: What do you call a blonde with half a brain?

A: *Gifted.*

Q: Why did the blonde put water on her computer?

A: *To wash the Windows.*

Q: What do you call it when a blonde dyes her hair brunette?

A: *Artificial intelligence.*

Q: What do dim lamps and blondes have in common?

A: *They both tend to be hot, but not too bright.*

Q: What's the difference between a blonde and a computer?

A: *You only have to punch information into a computer once.*

Q: Why did the blonde have a sore navel?

A: *Because her boyfriend was also blonde.*

Q: Why did the blonde go to the Apple Store?

A: *She wanted a Big Mac.*

Q: What's five miles long and has an IQ of forty?

A: *A blonde parade.*

Q: Did you hear about the blonde who tried to blow up her husband's car?

A: *She burned her lips on the tailpipe.*

Q: What's the difference between a blonde and a solar powered calculator?

A: *The blonde works in the dark.*

Q: What does a blonde do when her laptop computer freezes?

A: *She sticks it in the microwave.*

Q: What's the mating call of the blonde?

A: *"I'm sooooo drunk!"*

Q: What do you call ten blondes at the bottom of a pool?

A: *Air Pockets.*

Q: Did you hear about the blonde corn maze?
A: *It only had one stalk.*

Q: Why does a blonde keep ice cubes in the freezer?
A: *So she can keep the refrigerator cold.*

Q: What goes: vroooom-schreech, vrooom-schreech, vroooom-schreech?
A: *A blonde in a car at a flashing red light.*

Q: How do you know if a blonde has been sending e-mail?
A: *There is a bunch of envelopes stuffed into the disk drive.*

Q: Why did the blonde die in a helicopter crash?
A: *She got cold and turned off the ceiling fan.*

Q: Why did the blonde put sugar on her pillow?

A: *She wanted sweet dreams.*

Q: What was the blonde psychic's greatest achievement?

A: *An IN body experience.*

Q: Why did the blonde go outside with her purse open?

A: *Because she heard there would be a change in the weather.*

Q: Why did the blonde bring a pencil to her bedroom?

A: *She wanted to draw her curtains.*

Q: How do you brainwash a blonde?

A: *Give her a shower and then shake her upside down.*

Q: How do you measure a blonde's intelligence?

A: *Stick a tire pressure gauge in her ear.*

Q: Why do blondes hate Smarties?

A: *Because they're so hard to peel.*

Q: What do you get when you cross a blonde and a lawyer?

A: *I don't know; there are some things even a blonde won't do.*

Q: What's six inches long, has a bald head, and drives blondes crazy?

A: *A hundred dollar bill.*

Q: How do you keep a blonde busy?

A: *Write 'Please turn over' on both sides of a piece of paper.*

Q: What do you call a blonde with a runny nose?

A: *Full.*

Q: What does a blonde say when she gives birth?

A: *Are you sure it's mine?*

Q: How does a blonde car pool work?

A: *They all meet at work.*

Q: What does a blonde say when you ask her if her blinker is on?

A: *It's on. It's off. It's on. It's off. It's on. It's off.*

Q: What do you call ten blondes standing ear to ear?

A: *A wind tunnel.*

Q: Why did the blonde call the welfare office?

A: *She wanted to know how to cook food stamps.*

Q: Why don't blondes go bald?

A: *Because the vacuum in their head holds the hair in.*

Q: What do you call it when a blonde gets taken over by a demon?

A: *A vacant possession.*

Q: Why did the blonde return the jigsaw puzzle?

A: *She thought it was broken.*

Q: Why is it difficult for blonde girls to write the number 11?

A: *They never know which of the 1s comes first.*

Q: What did the blonde do when her boss gave her the pink slip?

A: *She wore it.*

Q: What is the difference between a blonde and an inflatable doll?

A: *About two cans of hair spray.*

Q: How many blondes does it take to play tag?

A: *One.*

Q: What's a blonde's favorite rock group?

A: *Air Supply.*

Q: What do you call four blondes lying on the ground?

A: *An air mattress.*

Q: What is a blonde's favorite part of a gas station?

A: *The Air Pump.*

Q: What's black and fuzzy and hangs from the ceiling?

A: *A blonde electrician.*

Q: Why is it okay for blondes to catch cold?

A: *They don't have to worry about blowing their brains out.*

Q: Why was the blonde running in circles around her bed?

A: *She was trying to catch up on her sleep.*

Q: Why can't you tell blondes knock-knock jokes?

A: *Because they go answer the door.*

Q: What do you call a blonde between two brunettes?

A: *A mental block.*

Q. What do you call a dumb blonde behind a steering wheel?

A. *An airbag.*

Q: What did the blonde do when her boyfriend was having a seizure in the bath tub?

A: *She threw in a load of laundry.*

Q: What do you call a blonde in a leather jacket?

A: *A rebel without a clue.*

Q: Why did the blonde only smell good on her right side?

A: *She didn't know where to buy Left Guard.*

Q: What did the blonde do when she noticed that someone had already written on the overhead transparency?

A: *She turned it over and used the other side.*

Q: What did the blonde name her pet zebra?

A: *Spot.*

Q: Why does the blonde leave the bathroom door open?

A: *Because somebody could be peeping at her through the keyhole.*

Q: What is the leading cause of death in blonde brain cells?

A: *Loneliness.*

Q: How do you keep a blonde busy?

A: *Write 'please turn over' on both sides of a piece of paper.*

Q: How do you keep a blonde in suspense?

A: *Give her a mirror and tell her to wait for the other person to say 'Hi.'*

Q: Why do blondes shower for hours?

A: *Because the shampoo bottle says, "Lather, rinse, and repeat."*

Q. What do you call a blonde in the closet?

A. *Last year's Hide 'n Seek champion.*

Q: What do you call a bunch of blondes standing in an empty area?

A: *A vacant lot.*

Q: What do you call a blonde with brain damage?

A: *Normal.*

Q: Why did the blonde law student keep failing her bar exam?

A: *She thought an anti-trust suit was a chastity belt.*

Q: Why do blondes have big belly-buttons?

A: *From dating blonde men.*

Q: Why was the blonde disappointed?

A: *Because she found out that 'Phillips 14 inch' was a TV.*

Q: What do you call a blonde with 2 brain cells?

A: *Pregnant.*

Q: Why did the blonde take a camera to bed?

A: *To record what she was going to dream that night.*

Q: Why did the blonde only tie one shoe?

A: *Because on the bottom it said "Taiwan" (Tie one).*

Q. Why does it take so long for a blonde to make chocolate chip cookies?

A. *She has to peel the M & M's.*

Q. Why do blondes wear ponytails?

A. *To hide the valve stem in the back of their necks.*

Q. What is the similarity between a smart blonde, Santa and the tooth fairy?

A. *They are all make-believe.*

Q: How do you erase a blonde's memory?

A: *Blow in her ear.*

Q: Why was the blonde confused after giving birth to twins?

A: *She couldn't figure out who the other mother was.*

Q: What did Star Trek's Bones McCoy say before he performed brain surgery on a blonde crew member?

A: *Space. The final frontier.*

Q: What did the blonde rush to the department store?

A: *She heard that men's pants were half off.*

Q. How do you keep a blonde at home?

A. *Build a circular driveway.*

Q: Why did the blonde want a test tube baby?

A: *So she could have a womb with a view.*

Q: Did you hear about the blonde who stayed up all night to see where the sun went?

A: *It finally dawned on her.*

Q: What did the blonde say when her doctor told her that she was pregnant?

A: *Is it mine?*

Q: What do you call an unmarried blonde in a BMW?

A: *A divorcee.*

Q: Why was the blonde late for work?

A: *She was stranded on the broken escalator.*

Q: What does a blonde say when you blow in their ear?

A: *"Thanks for the refill."*

Q: What does an intelligent blonde and a UFO have in common?

A: *No matter how often you hear about them, you never see one.*

Q. Why did the blonde got to the dentist?

A. *She wanted wisdom teeth put in.*

Chapter 3: Shorter Blonde Jokes

First Blonde: What does IDK stand for?

Second Blonde: I don't know.

First Blonde: Why doesn't anyone know?

A blonde drove to the shopping mall and found a parking spot which had a sign that read "1 Hour Only," but she wanted 2 hours to shop so she parked across 2 spaces.

A blonde was bragging about her knowledge of state capitals. She said to her friend, "Go ahead, ask me. I know all of them."

Her friend says, "OK then, what's the capital of Wisconsin?"

The blonde replies, "Oh, that's easy. W."

A blonde goes to her doctor and says that every time she drinks a coffee her eye hurts. The doctor prepared her a hot, fresh cup of coffee to see what really happens. She took a sip of the coffee and screamed, "Ouch that hurts!" The doctor said, "I know your problem." The blonde asked, "Is it bad, doctor?" The doctor replied, "No, you just need to take your spoon out of your cup before you drink your coffee."

A blonde came up to the librarian and said, "This book sucks. There are way too many people in it and the story makes no sense." The librarian said, "Oh, so you're the one who took our phone book."

A blonde is swimming in a river. A man walks up and asks her, "What are you doing in there?" She says, "I'm washing my clothes." The man asks, "Why don't you use a washing machine?" The blonde says, "I tried that, but it was too dizzy.

Blonde: "What is the second to last letter of the alphabet?

Redhead: "Y."

Blonde: "Because I want to know. Why do you have to question everything?"

A blonde decided to paint a room.

When her husband got home, he asked, "Why are you wearing a ski jacket and a winter coat?"

She replied, "The instructions on the paint can said 'For best results apply 2 coats.'"

One blonde was on one side of the river and there was another blonde on the other side of the river. One blonde yells to the other blonde, "How do you get to the other side?" and the other blonde yells back, "You are on the other side!"

A police officer sees a blonde woman crying under a street lamp on the sidewalk. He asks her what's wrong and if there's anything he can do to help. The blonde replies, "I lost my wedding ring." The officer asks, "Okay, where did you drop it?" The blonde says, "About a block away, but the light is better here."

Blonde: "Today must be Sunday."

Brunette: "Why?"

Blonde: "Because the sun is up."

A blonde fell and hurt herself at work. The doctor said she was and would be fine, but needed a little time to heal. The doctor suggested an easier job for a week or so. She brought the doctor's note to her boss and he suggested light duty for the week. The blonde began to cry. Her boss asked why she was crying. She said, "I don't know how to change lights."

Teacher: "If Astronomy is the name for the study of celestial objects, what would you call a person who studies the stars?"

Blonde student: "Paparazzi!"

Two blondes were walking in the park. The first blonde said, "Hey, look at that dog with one eye," so the second blonde covered up one eye and looked at it.

A blonde woman won horse riding lessons. Knowing nothing about riding but wanting to be properly dressed, she went out and bought riding boots. On the day of the first lesson, she showed up wearing only the riding boots. When asked why she was naked except for the boots, she said that she was told it was bareback riding and she didn't have any clothes that just covered the front.

A blonde guy marries his blonde girlfriend. On their first honeymoon night and the man doesn't quite know what to do. He calls his dad, who says, "Son, you take the hardest thing you got and you put it where she goes to the bathroom." The newlywed blonde guy thanks his father, hangs up the phone, and places his bowling ball in the toilet.

Brunette: "I found a condom on my patio last night."

Blonde: "What's a patio?"

A blonde painted an X on the bottom of the boat. Her blonde friend asked, "What are you doing?"

She replied, "Now I'll be able to find the same fishing spot again."

The other blonde called her an idiot saying, "But we may not get the same boat again."

A blonde had a near death experience yesterday when she went horseback riding.

Everything was going well until the horse started moving up and down.

She tried to hang on, but was thrown off. As she did, her foot got caught in the stirrup and she fell head first to the ground.

Her head kept bouncing as the horse carried on – it did not stop or even slow down.

Just as she was about to lose consciousness, the Wal-Mart manager came to the rescue and unplugged it.

A dumb blonde died and went to Heaven. When she got to the Pearly Gates, she met Saint Peter who said, "Before you get to come into Heaven, you have to pass a test."

"Oh, no!" she said.

A beggar walked up to a well-dressed blonde woman shopping on Rodeo Drive and said, "I haven't eaten anything in four days."

She looked at him and said, "God, I wish I had your willpower."

Three women, a blonde, a brunette and a redhead competed in the breast stroke division of a swimming competition.

The brunette came in first, and the redhead was a close second. Much later, the blonde finished, completely exhausted and near the point of drowning.

After being revived with blankets and coffee, she muttered, "I don't want to sound like a sore loser, but I think those other two girls cheated and used their arms."

A blonde and a redhead go to the beach. The blonde tells the redhead not to bother with the suntan oil.

The redheads ask her why, and the blonde replies, "I've drunk two bottles of it and I'm still as white as a sheet."

Two blondes are in a dark theatre.

The first blonde says, "The guy next to me is jerking off."

The other replies, "Just ignore him."

The first blonde says, "I can't. He's using my hand."

A blonde walked into a hardware store, picked up the hinges she was looking for, and went to go and pay for them.

The clerk asked her, "Need a screw for those hinges?"

She replied, "No, but how about a blow job for the socket set?"

Teacher: "Have you ever read Shakespeare?"

Blonde: "No, who wrote it?"

A beggar walked up to a well-dressed blonde woman shopping on Rodeo Drive and said, "I haven't eaten anything in four days."

She looked at him and said, "God, I wish I had your willpower."

Three women were at the gynaecologist having pre-natal check-ups. The doctor asked the first woman in what position was the baby conceived.

"He was on top," she replied.

"You will have a boy." the doctor told her.

The second woman was asked the same question.

"I was on top," she replied.

"You will have a baby girl." said the doctor.

With this, the third women, a blonde, burst into tears.

"What's the matter?" asked the doctor.

The blonde sobbed, "Am I going to have puppies?"

A doctor took up his stethoscope and said to his adolescent blonde patient: "Big breaths."

She replied: "Thanks, they always have been."

Three blondes are attempting to change a light bulb. One of them decides to call 911 for help.

Blonde: We need help. We're three blondes changing a light bulb.

Operator: Hmmm. You put in a fresh bulb?

Blonde: Yes.

Operator: Is the power in the house on?

Blonde: Of course.

Operator: Is the light switch on?

Blonde: Yes.

Operator: And the bulb still won't light up?

Blonde: No, it's working fine.

Operator: Then what's the problem?

Blonde: We got dizzy spinning the ladder around and we all fell and hurt ourselves.

A blonde was driving when she saw another blonde out in a field in a boat rowing.

The blonde stopped her car, got out and yelled, "You silly fool, it's blondes like you that give all us blondes a bad name. If I could swim I would come out there and give you what's coming to you."

A blonde guy and a brunette girl were happily married and about to have a baby.

One day, the wife started having contractions, so the husband rushed her to the hospital. He held her hand as she went through a trying birth. In the end, there were two little baby boys.

The blonde guy turned to his wife and angrily said, "All right, who's the other father?"

A woman's first pregnancy had produced twins.

With considerable pride she was telling her blonde friend how this happened once in every 10,000 times.

The blonde's eyes widened as she said, "It beats me how you ever found time to do any housework at all."

Teller: "Why did the blonde move to L.A.?"

Blonde: "I don't know. Why?"

Teller: "It was easier to spell."

Blonde: "Easier than what?"

A blonde was walking along, when she looked up to observe a bird flying overhead.

Suddenly, the bird drops a load when it was directly over her.

The blonde said to herself, "It's a good thing that cows don't fly."

A husband says to his blonde wife, "I thought we were going to have rice with the meat?"

His blonde wife replies, "That's right, but the cooking instructions for the rice said I needed 8 cups of water and there are only 6 cups in the cupboard."

A British Airways employee took a call from a blonde asking the question, "How long is the flight from London to New York?"

"Um, just a minute" he said.

Then, as he turned to check the exact flight time, he heard the blonde say, "Thank you," as the phone went dead.

A blonde guy was sitting in a bar when he spots a very pretty young woman. He advances towards her when the bartender says to him, "Don't waste your time on that one. She's a lesbian."

The blonde goes over to her anyway and says, "So which part of Lesbia are you from?"

A cop saw a young blonde woman down on her knees under a streetlight. "Can I help you?" he asked.

The woman replied, "I dropped my diamond ring and I'm looking for it."

The cop asked, "Did you drop it right here?"

"No," responded the blonde, "I dropped it about a block away, but the light's better here."

Three blondes walked into a bar and shouted, "We're not dumb! We put this puzzle together!"

The bartender said, "So what's the point?

The blondes said, "This puzzle says 3-5 years but we did it in 8 days."

One day a blonde is sitting in a bar trying to spear the olive in her drink with a toothpick, but the olive always eluded her. Finally a guy sitting next to the blonde picked up a toothpick and said "Here this is how you do it" and neatly speared the olive. "Big deal" said the blonde "I already had him so tired he couldn't get away."

A blonde walks into a bar with a door under her arm

"What's with the door?" asked the barman

"Well," said the blonde "its' a safety precaution; last night I lost my key."

"What happens if you lose the door?" asked the barman.

"That's alright, I left the window open" replied the blonde.

Two blondes walk into a bar that serves food and pull out their sandwiches. The barman tells them "You can't eat your own sandwiches in here." So they swapped.

Two drunk guys came out of a bar. One looked up and said, "That's the moon." The other one said, "No it's not, that's the sun." They were arguing back and forth until this blonde came up. They asked her what it was and she said, "I don't know, I'm not from around here."

A blonde walks into a bar and orders 18 beers. "Why so many?" asked the bartender. "Can't you read the sign?" replied the blonde "no one served under 18."

While on holiday a blonde rushes into an English pub and shouts, "Help; my mother-in-law has sunk up to her ankles in the bog on the moors."

"Not to worry," replied a local "as soon as I finish this drink I'll come and help you."

The blonde decides that she might as well have a drink too while she waits.

"I think she's probably up to her knees by now," said the local when he finally finished his drink.

"I'm not sure," said the blonde "I forgot to mention that she went in head first."

A blonde approaches a stranger and asks what time it is. The stranger says, "11:45." The blonde says, "Really? That's so weird. Every time I ask that question, I get a different answer."

A man is sitting on his porch when he notices two blondes working down the road. They both have shovels. One of them digs a hole and the other immediately fills it in. The man watches them for an hour and finally approaches them, "You look like you're working hard. But I'm not sure what you're trying to accomplish."

One of the blondes replies, "Well there's usually three of us, but the one that plants the trees is sick."

A man goes to a coffee shop and asks the blonde waitress, "Can I have a coffee with sugar, no cream?"

The waitress replies, "Oh, I'm sorry sir but we don't have cream. Could I get it to you with no milk instead?"

A brunette asked a blonde scuba diver why they jumped off the boat backwards.

The blonde replied, "Duh. If I jumped forwards I would still be in the boat."

Chapter 4: Longer Blonde Jokes

The Exam

The blonde reports for the first part of her college examination which consists of "Yes/No" type questions.

She takes her seat in the examination hall, stares at the question paper for five minutes, and then in a moment of inspiration she takes her purse out, removes a coin and starts tossing the coin into the air and then marking the answer sheet - Yes for Heads and No for Tails.

Within an hour she is all done whereas the rest of the class is sweating it out.

During the last few minutes, she is seen desperately throwing the coin, muttering and swearing.

The moderator, alarmed, approaches her and asks what is going on.

She replied, "I finished the exam in forty minutes, and I'm just re-checking my answers."

At The Carnival

A young blonde woman is asked out on a date and accepts. The boy picks her up and they go to a nearby carnival in town. They ride a few rides, play a few games, and seem to be generally hitting it off well. The boy asks her, "What do you want to do now?"

"I want a weigh," she says.

Well, OK, thinks the boy. They walk over to the fortune scales, and weigh her. They play a few more games and stop for food.

"What do you want to do now?" asks the boy.

"I want a weigh," she says.

Hmmm, a little odd but I'll put up with it, thinks the boy. Again they get her weight and fortune.

After yet another few games and an exquisite fireworks show, the boy asks, "What do you want to do now?"

"I want a weigh," she says.

Damn, thinks the boy, she's just too weird for me. They get her weight and fortune, and the boy drives her home.

As she walks into the house, her sister asks, "How did your date go?"

"Wousy," says the blonde.

The Headphones

A blonde walked into a hairdresser's with a pair of headphones on and asked the hairdresser for a haircut, but that the hairdresser mustn't touch her headphones.

"Fine" said the hairdresser, a little taken aback, but happy for the work.

A month later, the same blonde returned and asked for another haircut but with the same condition, "Whatever you do ... don't touch the headphones."

"No problem," said the hairdresser who went on to give her another good cut, considering the restraint.

Three weeks later, the blonde came in again, and once again she said, "Don't touch the headphones."

The hairdresser cut her hair, and on finishing, she couldn't resist and she just lifted one side of the headphones up.

The blonde promptly fell to the floor unconscious.

"Oh my God - I think I've killed her," screamed the hairdresser as she picked up the headphones and put them on herself.

She heard the strangest thing..."breathe in...breathe out...breathe in...breathe out."

The Hitchhiker

A truck driver was driving between towns on a country road when he spotted a gorgeous blonde hitchhiking at the side of the road.

He stopped without hesitation and the curvy blonde climbed into the cab showing mountains of cleavage

50 miles or so further down the road, he got a flat, so he pulled his truck to the side of the road and got out to inspect the tire.

He was fiddling around with the wheel, when the blonde opened the window and shouted down, "Do you want a screw driver?"

The driver replied, all smiles, "I might as well. I can't get this hub cap off."

Three Parachutes

A plane had four people in it: a lawyer, a teenage boy, a priest and a blonde girl. The pilot said that the plane was going to crash but there were only three parachutes.

The four passengers began discussing their predicament.

The blonde said, "I look beautiful so I should get one too" so she jumped off with one.

The lawyer said "I help people solve their problems so I should get one" so he jumped off with one. Now there were only two people left: a priest and the teenage boy.

The priest said to the boy "Here you take the last parachute and go because you will live a longer life then me."

However, the young boy said "No, it's all right because there are still two parachutes left. The blonde just took my backpack!"

Road Striping

A blonde, a brunette and a redhead all tried out for the same job as road stripers. The boss told them they would all work for two days and whoever painted the most would get the job.

At the end of the first day, the redhead had painted three miles, the brunette had painted four miles and the blonde had painted five miles.

The next day, the redhead painted three miles and the brunette four miles and the blonde just one mile.

The boss was disappointed; and he asked the blonde, "What went wrong, you were doing so well?"

The blonde replied, "Well, that bucket of paint just kept getting further and further away."

I Want To Buy A Television

A blonde walks into an electronics store to buy a television. She finds a salesman and tells him, "I want to buy this television," as she points. The salesman tells her, "Sorry but we don't sell televisions to blondes."

The girl walks out and walks back inside five minutes later with a brunette wig. She finds another salesman and tells him, "Sir, I want to buy this television," as she points. The salesman tells her, "Sorry but we don't sell televisions to blondes."

She leaves and comes back once again, but this time with a red wig on. Sure that a clerk would sell her the TV this time, she returns and asks a different clerk this time.

To her astonishment, this clerk also says that she doesn't serve blondes. The blonde asks the clerk, "How in the world do you know I am a blonde?"

The clerk looks at her wincingly and says, "That's not a TV madam; it's a microwave."

Ice Fishing

A blonde wanted to go ice fishing. She'd seen a few books on the subject, and after getting all the necessary items together, she decided to give it a go. After positioning her footstool, she started to make a circular cut in the ice.

Unexpectedly, a voice boomed, "There are no fish under the ice."

Alarmed, the blonde looks around but as she can't see anybody, she continues fishing. Again, from the heavens, the voice bellowed, "There are no fish under the ice."

The blonde, now quite worried, moved way down to the opposite end of the ice, sat up her stool, and tried again to cut her hole. The voice came once more: "There are no fish under the ice."

She stopped, looked to the skies, and exclaimed, "Is that you, Lord?"

The voice replied, "No, I'm the Ice-Rink Manager!"

Bottom Deodorant

The blonde walks into a drugstore and asks the pharmacist for some bottom deodorant. The pharmacist, a little bemused, explains to the woman that they don't sell anything called bottom deodorant, and never have.

Unfazed, the blonde assures him that she has been buying the stuff from this store on a regular basis, and would like some more. "I'm sorry," says the pharmacist, "we don't have any."

"But I always get it here," says the blonde.

"Do you have the container it comes in?"

"Yes!" says the blonde, "I will go and get it."

She returns with the container and hands it to the pharmacist, who looks at it and says to her, "This is just a normal stick of underarm deodorant."

The annoyed blonde snatches the container back and reads out loud from the container: "To apply, push up bottom."

Interrogation

A policeman was interrogating three blondes who were training to become detectives. To test their skills in recognizing a suspect, he shows the first blonde a picture. "This is your suspect, how would you recognize him?" The first blonde answers, "That's easy, we'll catch him quickly because he only has one eye."

The policeman says, "That's because the picture shows his profile." He shows the picture to the second blonde and asks her, "This is your suspect; how would you recognize him?" The second blonde giggles, flips her hair and says, "Ha. He'd be easy to catch because he only has one ear." The policeman responds, "What's the matter with you two? Of course there is only one eye and one ear showing as it is a picture of his profile."

He shows the picture to the third blonde and asks, "This is your suspect; how would you recognize him?" The blonde looks at the picture and says, "The suspect obviously wears contact lenses." The policeman is confused, and says, "Wait here a few minutes while I check his file." He leaves the room and goes to his office, checks the suspect's file in his computer, and comes back with a beaming smile on his face. "Wow. You're right, the suspect does in fact wear contact lenses. That's very good detective work. How were you able to make such an astute observation?"

"That's easy," the blonde replied. "He can't wear a pair of glasses because he only has one eye and one ear."

Tickle Me Elmo

A blonde woman applied for a job at the factory where they make the "Tickle-Me-Elmo" dolls.

The boss told her to report for work on Monday and explained that she would be stationed on the assembly line just before the dolls were packed into boxes.

On Monday morning they started up the production line and within fifteen minutes had to shut it down because one worker couldn't keep up.

The boss went down the line to find the problem.

He saw that it was the new blonde worker who couldn't keep up.

The blonde was very busy trying to do her part but she had a bunch of dolls waiting for her.

Closer examination showed that she was sewing little cloth bags containing two walnuts in the appropriate place on the dolls.

When the boss could control his laughter he said, "Lady, I said to give each doll two test-tickles."

New Cabin Crew

An airline captain was breaking in a new blonde stewardess. The route they were flying had a layover in another city.

Upon their arrival, the captain showed the stewardess the best place for airline personnel to eat and shop.

The next morning, as the pilot was preparing the crew for the day's route, he noticed the new stewardess was missing.

He knew which room she was in at the hotel and he called her up to find out what had happened.

She answered the phone, crying, and said she couldn't get out of her room.

"You can't get out of your room?" the captain asked, "Why not?"

The blonde stewardess replied, "There are only three doors in here," she sobbed, "one is the bathroom, one is the closet, and one has a sign on it that says 'Do Not Disturb'."

Car Repair

A blonde was driving home after a game and got caught in a really bad hailstorm. Her car was covered with dents, so the next day she took it to a repair shop.

The shop owner saw that she was a blonde, so he decided to have some fun. He told her just to go home and blow into the tail pipe really hard, and all the dents would pop out.

So, the blonde went home, got down on her hands and knees and started blowing into her tailpipe. Nothing happened. So she blew a little harder, and still nothing happened.

Her blonde roommate came home and said, "What are you doing?"

The first blonde told her how the repairman had instructed her to blow into the tail pipe in order to get all the dents to pop out.

The roommate rolled her eyes and said, "Uh, like hello. You need to roll up the windows first."

The Eye Test

A blonde went to an optician to have her eyes checked for glasses.

She was directed to read various letters with her left eye while covering her right eye.

The blonde got so mixed up on which eye was which that the optician took a paper bag with a hole to see through, and covered up the appropriate eye for her.

As he did so, he noticed the blonde had tears streaming down her face.

The optician said, "There's no need to get emotional about getting glasses."

"I know," agreed the blonde, "But I kind of had my heart set on wire frames."

Early Finish

A blonde, a brunette, and a redhead all work at the same office for a female boss who always goes home early.

One day the brunette says, "Hey girls, let's go home early tomorrow. She'll never know."

So the next day, they all leave right after the boss does.

The brunette gets some extra gardening done, the redhead goes to a bar, and the blonde goes home to find her husband having sex with the female boss!

She quietly sneaks out of the house, goes shopping and returns home at her normal time.

The next day the brunette says. "We should do it again sometime."

"No way," says the blonde. "I almost got caught."

Men In Trench Coats

A blonde's car breaks down so she eases it over onto the shoulder of the road. She carefully steps out of the car and opens the trunk.

Out jump two men in trench coats who walk to the rear of the vehicle where they stand facing oncoming traffic and begin opening their coats and exposing their nude bodies to approaching drivers.

A huge pileup occurs with multiple car crashes.

It's not very long before a police car shows up. The cop, clearly enraged, runs towards the broken down vehicle and yells, "What the hell is going on here?"

"My car broke down," says the blonde calmly.

"Well, what are these perverts doing here by the road?" asks the cop.

The blonde replies, "Those are my emergency flashers."

Alligator Shoes

A blonde woman goes to a shoe store in Louisiana wanting to buy some alligator shoes, but becomes irritated when she sees the price.

She walks out of the store saying, "I'm going to catch an alligator and get my own pair of shoes." The shopkeeper laughs as he watches her leave.

Later as the shopkeeper is driving home, he sees the blonde in a swamp by the side of the road.

A six foot alligator is swimming right at her but she swiftly knocks the creature out. She drags it onto some grass where there are a few other knocked out alligators.

She flips it over on its back, and frustrated, shouts out, "Damn it, this one isn't wearing any shoes either."

Snowed In

A man and his blonde wife are sitting inside, by the fire, when the radio announcer comes on: "We are expecting up to a foot of snow tonight, please make sure you are parked on the even-numbered side of the road." The wife goes out and moves her car.

The next day the same thing happens, and the announcer comes on and says: "We are expecting up to a foot of snow tonight, please make sure you are parked on the odd-numbered side of the road." The wife goes out and moves her car.

A few days later the same thing happens and the announcer comes on: "We are expecting up to two feet of snow tonight, please make sure you are parked on the-" but the power goes out in the middle of the announcement.

The blonde freaks out and screams, "Which side do I put my car on?"

Her husband tenderly comforts her saying, "How about we just leave the car in the garage this time?"

Chapter 5: Rude Blonde Q&A Jokes

Please do not be offended by these rude jokes. If you think you will be, please stop reading now.

Q. Why don't blondes eat bananas?

A. *They can't find the zipper.*

Q: Why don't blondes like anal sex?

A: *They don`t like their brains being screwed with.*

Q: How do you get a blonde pregnant?

A: *Come in her shoes and let the flies do the rest.*

Q: Why are blonde's coffins Y-shaped?

A: *Because as soon as they are on their backs, their legs open.*

Q: Why do blondes wear panties?

A: *To keep their ankles warm.*

Q: What's the difference between a corn farmer with epilepsy and a blonde with diarrhoea?

A: *One shucks between fits.*

Q: How is a blonde like a postage stamp?

A: *You lick them, stick them, and send them on their way.*

Q: What does a blonde and a tornado have in common?

A: *At first there's a lot of sucking and blowing and then you lose your house.*

Q: What's the difference between a blonde and a walrus?

A: *One has whiskers and fishy flaps, and the other is a walrus.*

Q: Why did the blonde stop using birth control pills?

A: *Because they kept falling out.*

Q: Why is a blonde like a turtle?

A: *Once they're on their backs, they're screwed.*

Q: What's the difference between a blonde and an ironing board?

A: *It's difficult to open the legs of an ironing board.*

Q: What's the difference between a blonde and a guy?

A: *The blonde has the higher sperm count.*

Q: What do you call a blonde with a dollar on top of her head?

A: *All you can eat, under a buck.*

Q: What's the difference between a blonde and a lightbulb?

A: *The lightbulb is smarter, but the blonde is easier to turn on.*

Q: What does a blonde do when she reaches orgasm?

A: *She screams her own name.*

Q: What's a blonde's favorite nursery rhyme?

A: *Hump-me Dump-me.*

Q: What does a screen door and a blonde have in common?

A: *The more you bang it, the looser it gets.*

Q: How is a blonde's hair like her boyfriend's cock?

A: *They both get blown dry every day.*

Q: What is the difference between a blonde and a shower?

A: *A shower has to be turned on to get wet.*

Q: What do you call four blondes laying on a beach?

A: *Public access.*

Q: What do you call two blondes in a canoe?

A: *Fur traders.*

Q: How is a blonde like a vacuum cleaner?

A: *Turn her on and she starts to suck.*

Q: Why do blondes always drink with straws?
A: *For sucking practise.*

Q: Why do blondes like cars with tilt steering?
A: *More head room.*

Q: Why don't blondes talk during sex?
A: *Their mothers taught them never to speak to strangers.*

Q: Why don't blondes use vibrators?
A: *They would chip their teeth.*

Q: Why did the blonde finally pass her driving test?
A: *She took the examiner with her.*

Q: Why do blondes like cars with sunroofs?

A: *More leg room.*

Q: What do a blonde and an instant lottery ticket have in common?

A: *All you have to do is scratch the box to win.*

Q: What is the worst thing about sex with a blonde?

A: *Bucket seats.*

Q: Why is it a bad idea to let a blonde girl skydive when she's on her period?

A: *She will probably pull the wrong string.*

Q: Why are blondes so sexually promiscuous?

A: *Who cares?*

Q: What is 68 to a blonde?

A: *Where she goes down on you and you owe her one.*

Q: How do you know if a blonde has been using your game console?

A: *The joystick is soaking wet.*

Q: What's the definition of a metallurgist?

A: *Someone who can tell if a platinum blonde is a virgin metal or a common ore.*

Q: Why does NASA hire peroxide blondes?

A: *They're doing research on black holes.*

Q: How can you tell when a blonde reaches orgasm?

A: *The batteries have run out.*

Q: Why can't blondes be cattle ranchers?

A: *They can't even keep two calves together.*

Q: What nickname is most used by blondes?

A: *B.J.*

Q: What does a blonde do for foreplay?

A: *She removes her panties.*

Q: Why do blondes wear earmuffs?

A: *To avoid the draft.*

Q: Why are rectal thermometers banned for use in blondes?

A: *They cause too much brain damage.*

Q: How does a blonde do it doggy-style?

A: *She takes off her clothes and makes her boyfriend roll over and beg.*

Q: Why are blondes like pianos?

A: *When they aren't upright, they're grand.*

Q: What is the difference between blondes and some traffic signs?

A: *Some traffic signs say stop.*

Q: What did the blonde do to bring her golfer husband luck?

A: *She licked his balls.*

Q: What do you say to a blonde that won't come home with you?

A: *"Have another beer."*

Q: What's unique about a blonde's anatomy?

A: *There are no private parts.*

Q: Why did the blonde tattoo her zip-code on her thigh?

A: *She wanted a lot of male in her box.*

Q: How can you tell a blonde has had a bad day?

A: *Her tampon is behind her ear and she doesn't know what she did with her cigarette.*

Q: What does a blonde say after multiple orgasms?

A: *"Way to go team."*

Q: Why is a blonde like an old washing machine?

A: *They both drip when they're f*cked.*

Q: Why do blondes take birth control pills?
A: *So they know what day of the week it is.*

Q: Why is a blonde like a front door?
A: *They both have male slots.*

Q: How can you tell if a blonde has a vibrator?
A: *By the chipped tooth.*

Q: What do you call two nuns and a blonde?
A: *Two tight ends and a wide receiver.*

Q: What's the difference between a blonde and a mosquito?
A: *The mosquito stops sucking when you hit it.*

Q: Why did the blonde stick her boyfriend's cock in her ear?

A: *She wanted to try aural sex.*

Chapter 6: Rude Blonde Jokes

Please do not be offended by these rude jokes. If you think you will be, please stop reading now.

Three blondes had boyfriends all named Brad and they kept getting confused when they were talking to one another, so they decided to name each of their boyfriends after sodas.

The first blonde said, "I'll call my boyfriend 7 Up, because he's seven inches long and he's always up for it."

The second blonde said, "I'll call my boyfriend Mountain Dew, because he mounts me and he knows exactly what to do."

The third blonde said, "I'll call mine Jack Daniels."

The other two blondes looked at her and said, "You can't do that - that's not a soda; that's a hard licker."

A smile crossed the third blonde's face as she said, "I know."

Did you hear about the blonde bride that was so horny she carried a bouquet of batteries?

A blonde says to her friend, "It's embarrassing, but every time I sneeze, I have an orgasm."

Her friend asks, "What are you taking for it?"

The blonde replies, "Snuff."

A blonde came running downstairs, crying. Her mother asked what was wrong and the blonde said her boyfriend had just dumped her.

Her blonde mother nodded wisely and proceeded to tell her about the birds and the bees.

The blonde interrupted and said, "No, it's not that. I can f*ck and suck with the best of them. But he says I can't cook."

The farmer said to his blonde wife, "Let's have kids." The blonde agreed and ten minutes later she was screwing their goat.

A blonde friend of mine was looking for some transportation, so I bought her a Woody.

I called her up later and asked how she liked it.

She told me it was OK, but that it didn't look so good once she had taken it out of the crate.

A blonde goes into a drug store to buy some rubbers (so she can practice safe sex). She asks the pharmacist, "How much for a pack of rubbers?"

"They're two dollars for a pack of 3," he replied, "Plus 12 cents for the tax."

"Oh," said the blonde, "I wondered how they kept them on."

The blonde was so dumb she thought that condiment was a mint-flavored condom.

A blonde lay in her hospital bed recovering from an operation when the doctor cane by to check on her progress.

She asked him, "How soon before I can have sex again?"

The doctor replied, "I'm not sure. No-one has ever asked me that after a tonsillectomy before."

A man goes to confession and says to the priest, "Father, I have sinned. I slept with two blondes last week."

The priest says, "Go home, squeeze five lemons into a cup, and drink it really fast."

The man asks, "Will that absolve me of all my sins?" The priest says, "No. But it will wipe that smirk off your face."

My blonde girlfriend really wanted to win the double entendre competition this weekend, so I entered her.

A husband tells his hot blonde wife, "If you would learn to iron properly, we could do without the ironing lady."

The blonde wife replies, "Well, if you would learn to f*ck me properly, we could do without the gardener."

A blonde filled out a job application, and under 'Last Position' she wrote 'Doggy Style.'

Confucious say: 'Blonde who fly upside down have crack up.'

There was this blonde couple who were into S&M. He snores; she masturbates.

A blonde and a redhead are at work when the redhead gets a delivery of a dozen roses from her boyfriend.

She sighs and says, "Oh, no, my boyfriend is buying me flowers again."

The blonde looks quizzically at her and says, "Don't you like getting flowers?"

The redhead says, "I love getting flowers, but he always has expectations after giving me flowers, and I just don't feel like spending the next three days on my back with my legs in the air."

The blonde says, "Don't you have a vase?"

A blonde boasts to her girlfriend that her boyfriend is very thoughtful as he always clears the browser history so that they will have more space on their computer.

This guy had just started a new job working at a porno shop, and his boss had left him alone in the shop for a while.

Soon a white woman comes in and asks, "How much for the white dildo?"

He answers, "$50."

She: "How much for the black one?"

He: "$50 for the black one, $50 for the white one."

She: "I think I'll take the black one. I've never had a black one before."

She pays him, and off she goes.

A little later a black woman comes in and asks "How much for the black dildo?"

He: "$50."

She: "How much for the white one?"

He: "$50 for the white one, $50 for the black one."

She: "I think I'll take the white one. I've never had a white one before."

She pays him, and off she goes.

A little later a blonde woman comes in and asks, "How much are your dildos?"

He: "$50 for the white one, $50 for the black one."

She: "Well, how much is that tartan one on the shelf?"

He: "Well, that's a very special dildo and it'll cost you $145."

She thinks for a moment and answers, "I'll take the tartan one; I've never had a tartan one before."

The blonde pays him, and off she goes.

When the guy's boss returns he asks, "How did you do while I was gone?"

The salesman responded, "I did really well, I sold one white dildo, one black dildo, and I sold your thermos for $145!"

Chapter 7: You Know You Are A Blonde If...

You know you are a blonde if you think a G-string is part of a violin.

You know you are a blonde if you believe menopause is a button on the remote control.

You know you are a blonde if you think pubic hair is a wild rabbit in the Outback.

You know you are a blonde if you believe 'Spread Eagle' is an extinct bird.

You know you are a blonde if you think anus is the Latin word for yearly.

You know you are a blonde if you believe testicles are found on an octopus.

You know you are a blonde if you believe a diaphragm is a drawing in geometry.

You know you are a blonde if you believe genitals are people of non-Jewish origins.

You know you are a blonde if you don't know what "too much pink" means.

You know you are a blonde if your blood type is glitter.

You know you are a blonde if teachers don't waste time trying to educate you.

You know you are a blonde if you believe shopping burns calories.

You know you are a blonde if you don't have too many clothes, and not enough closets.

You know you are a blonde if your greatest fear is wearing a cute outfit on an insignificant day.

You know you are a blonde if you go to the dentist to get your Bluetooth fixed.

You know you are a blonde if you don't see the world in black and white, but in pink and glitter.

You know you are a blonde if you're a walking punchline.

You know you are a blonde if you think an umbilical cord is part of a parachute.

You know you are a blonde if you think about why the walls at Walgreens aren't green.

Chapter 8: Pick-Up Lines To Use On Blondes

Is it hot in here, or is it you?

I've just put you on top of my 'to-do' list.

I'm not very tall. I'm just sitting on my wallet.

I am curious – are you as good as all the guys say you are?

Oh damn, I just dropped the keys to my Porsche.

Did you know your hair and my pillow are perfectly color co-ordinated?

I am an undertaker, and I have a stiff one that needs dealing with urgently.

I'm a great swimmer. Shall I demonstrate the breast stroke with you?

I'm a doctor and I'm here to offer you a free mammogram.

I'm feeling a little off. Would you mind turning me on?

If you were an ice lolly, I would be licking you all night long.

If being sexy was a crime, you'd be guilty.

Hey baby, want to see my elephant?

I'm no Fred Flintstone, but I can make your Bedrock.

Nice dress. Can I talk you out of it?

I'm a bird watcher and I'm looking for a big breasted bed thrasher.

Can I add a branch to your family tree?

Do you sleep on your stomach? If not, can I?

If I told you that you have a nice body, would you hold it against me?

What do you like for breakfast?

There's a party in my mouth. Do you want to come?

Are we related? Do you want to be?

Did you get your jeans in a sale? Because at my place they are 100% off.

Are you doing anything tonight, because I sure hope it's me.

Do you want to see something swell?

Is that a ladder in your tights, or is it a stairway to heaven?

Why don't you sit on my lap, and we'll talk about the first thing that pops up.

You smell wet. Let's party.

Chapter 9: About the Author

Charlie Crapper has written a number of funny joke books and was recently named Most Promising Comedy Writer Of The Year by the International Jokers Guild. It is fair to say that his blonde friends; and one in particular, has provided him with plenty of material for this blondes joke book.

He firmly believes that "Blondes Have More Fun" and that "Gentlemen Prefer Blondes" and he hopes that you enjoyed this collection of blonde jokes. As you know, some of the gags were tongue in cheek, but hopefully the book brought a smile to your face.

If you saw anything wrong, or you have a gag you would like to see included in the next version of this book, please visit the glowwormpress.com website.

If you did enjoy the book, kindly leave a review on Amazon so that others can enjoy a good laugh too.

Final Gag:-

Q: What is the definition of the perfect woman?

A: A blonde nymphomaniac whose father owns a bar.

Printed in Great Britain
by Amazon